The King of Prussia Is Drunk on Stars

Marc Vincenz

Lavender Ink
New Orleans

The King of Prussia Is Drunk on Stars
by Marc Vincenz
Copyright © 2024 by Marc Vincenz and Lavender Ink
All rites reserved. No part of this work may be reproduced, etc.

Cover image by Edmund Weiß, 1888, from E. Weiß, *Bilderatlas der Sternenwelt.*
It depicts the Leonid Meteor Storm, as seen over North America in 1833.
Cover design: Marc Vincenz
Book design: F. J. Bergmann and Marc Vincenz
Author portrait and gecko by Sophia Santos

Library of Congress Control Number: 2023947135
Vincenz, Marc
The King of Prussia Is Drunk on Stars / Marc Vincenz
p. cm.
ISBN 978-1-956921-22-9 (paperback)

Lavender Ink
New Orleans
lavenderink.org
ᘁᘁ

for Franz Schlögel, in memoriam

Table of Contents

THE GREAT WAVE OF HAIR

MORE NAKED TRUTHS

FRANZL ON THE MOONSOAKED PATH

FRANZ LASHED TO THE RAILROAD TRACKS

vii

The King
of Prussia
Is Drunk on Stars

Five-Star Liquor ★★★★★

When were you going to tell me
everything finally ends up in the sky?

Split Your Skull, Monster

Keep to the road, dear soul.
The sidewalks are splattered with dead letters.

I learned where you should wind up—
the door was clearly unlocked.
Still, I kicked it open.

You have a monstrous way about you,
but you wear it well.
You have patches of tar and pitch;
wires popping out here and there.

Still, no tune is new,
summer has forgotten us
with her brown cows on the hill,
all those green slopes up there,
the warmed bats in their evening formations.

And in the race ahead,
do you think you can
still match his stride?

I know you enjoyed it all night long.

Many rarer rivers meet by their own hand.

Shards of Air

Take the mountain chains where the golden plover has arrived, run your fingers down the grassy green slopes. The shore near the river is green too. Somehow last year's leaves still hang on in the cracks and crevices; they tremble, they're awestruck and terrified as the river churns. But here in the city, pressed against a wall, all your features blur, and yet somehow the serene cool green lingers—if only you could drift slowly into the eddy. Irony of ironies, as you stop to gather your thoughts under the gaze of a glossy metal highrise, you wish for a handful of wildflowers.

4

Bare-Bones Silence

That word, *forever,*
seemed inaudible.

Bundled in our coats,
we were quite the picture.

The powers have sobered,
as they say. Foolish to think

that everything scurries off
into eternity. A father's

letter may lie heavy,
and you were holding on

to his every last word
while all this escaped me.

If it were my death tonight,
all those old taboos

would melt into my skin
in their hunt for meaning,

in their hunt for the stillness
to carry me   over the rapids ... ★

From a Hotel Window

[Something floral here] ...

Draw apart in two, in the bright blood of the bright word, Sister
Rachel of the coronary arteries, you are the light! Each barb of
wire, each eyeless, formless figure moves you toward life.

A homeland has no second thoughts,

[Something about a simmering instruction here] ...

We renounced the light until it fell over us,
all fluorescence.

Did you recognize the man in the poster?

Upward of Ten

What unsuitable accommodations!
This she said in her human fashion, inflamed.

A shrub leaf she remained
until the heavens opened.

Conscience

Where we have been:
in the spinning of the waterwheels?

Or the one that seizes up
on your watch, swept away?

(I don't need you niggling.
I do that enough myself.)

(Really? When were you the wind?
Oh, and you meant to sail me to the ends.)

The scale of courage? Unfathomable.

(Those words spoken on the bluff in the screeching rain.)

Where have you been
in all that spinning water?

Mostly the unseen or the illegible?

Concave, this canvas, and filled with uncountable atoms.

A bear eats an apple core.
A dog gets away with it.

A Handful of Rice for Sigurður Jonsson

Partly your friend or what you take away from it;
it's so true it sways in you, the fate of it; hold on—
with every breath it takes for it, the truth of it;

how dare you step away from me
in these burning woods, that light hemp bag
of fish bones you carry on your back—

from behind we can see all of it: aggressive,
that Viking raven on the wall, on the lights
up there or the burning down here. Meanwhile,

shored up, you lie there like always.
Good to see you too. Cut all those ties and sway.
See: the table is laden with gifts

from Grindavik to Mosfellsbaer.
Odin would say we shouldn't indulge
in all this self-pity. No time is right.

Trash Nebula

Would you throw a ball?
A stone cast, and all that,
into a small objective world?

So you were back then,
then you darkened in a pall,
only a chalk trace

left on the earth.
Fill in all the wilderness,
will you. I know:

Love me in one death.

This night-glazed invasion
underswept those with us
and those against

(I can tell you it was 4 to 1).

At the vacant center,
unleavened and leavened,
disks of scrap, skyward bright,
`
followed you—
those little bits of iron
ore, magnetized with songs of praise.

No, we were not satisfied.

Don't be extinguished;
your house, after all,

was a budding train
noontime and night.

Even you stand
with open eyes;

no, it's evening,
right? We could not

deter you to cast
the unused
          over the shoulder—

with salt it brings luck—
but when were you
          going to tell me

II

everything finally
ends up in the sky?

Riptide

Squared away.
Floored in wooden clogs.

What nibbles?

See that signpost over there?
That's all he can do.
He sits on the ice, perched over his small fish.

He knows who's biting
and waits alone.

A Confession of Sorts

The grandmother-babbles
are hard to fathom.

What folly from that shorthand,
the directions played,
the herd thinned out.

Who made them then,
when there is no wind left?

From childhood we looked out
into the softness of the world;

the remains, though, were exhumed
and entombed—every prophecy worms

its way through the knots and gnarls
(that's where the scars come from).

And yes, Rosalie and I drank the sun
in the chicken yard, then stopped

the fountain from spurting-
sputtering in the light.

Franz Overlooking the Mountain

At night the wind fights
its own hidden meaning.

Machine

Philomela. Seductoro. Illuminatrix. Divine with dignity.

When I was young I would look at myself as a panther in the moneytree. I know that's a tall order, but would you rather join the haystack? Being that singular key where thoughts roam free. The cat is in the bag.

More than anyone in the known history of this planet, she finds strength even down that steep cliff. Yes, it's a dream we carry.

Culture

When All Is Said and Done

A sudden hidden meaning,
droplets to the east wind
liberated as pieces with hidden meaning.

Heave-ho, Li Po,
a foreign wind has stirred the horsemen,
liberated as pieces of a stormcloud:

Reading too much.
But I keep at it; at night, the wind
is liberated in its own hidden meaning.

All those prophecies
drunk on stars, the floodlights of the fjord,
and liberated by water rushing in its intensity.

Surge of strife, dry seasons,
a galaxy of the infinite, a seasoned
fright slips through the liberated branches.

A droplet—don't think too much—
gather the firewood and liberate the water.
Lie there, wet and gleaming black. Don't look back.

At Home Over the Road

Oxygenated verse. Pop its cork.
See not what you see in the darkness;
see yourself holding the candle—honestly.

The mergers and acquisitions sit
in their crates, all of them shoulder to shoulder;
how does the breeze make it through the thicket?

Along the hung wares of the spider,
who would dare to see it as we imagine?
Would you wash inside, sir?

Not cast for her, but their heir,
those cold excursions in the eye of the moon,
where moths have settled in their vestigial doom.

19

For a Long Time Ago

The bullfinch flies out
from under the apple tree, singing in short bursts
as her partner steals buds.

The monkey says, The old tiger slinks
through the grass holding a star in her mouth.
Shall he dare the leap into the forest.

The watering hole at dusk is bone dry.
Who shoulders all these grains of sand?
Shoot for the mountain, my mother always said.

Never quite acquired that regal majesty.
While you're at it, my grandfather said,
will you hand me the hammer?

This side of me, miles and miles of it,
a future with confidence, then suddenly
a wave of sorrow curls up at my feet.

Winter mornings I throw crusts for the birds;
the forest is still silent beneath the stars,
a lion tiptoes into a land made of meat.

Dead wasps on the windowsills, someone haunts
this house besmitten, someone else
plays the cello. He's a man just like you.

Birth of a Nation

Keep your head, or so it was said when there were
guillotines. On the other hand, they said,
find the confidence in your tongue.

This side of the war is peaceful.
All the world's diamonds, miles of them,
repeat, one eye glaring into another's dreams.

The ground is saying, don't stop!
Keep on walking until the leaves change color.
Now black and blue, they burn into earth.

Baking Bread

Cooking something up after midnight.
Stirring a potent brew. Omens. For whom
the bell tolls, and so on and so forth.

To grasp the mouse in all of its shrieking fury,
to shudder at the screech of a bat, to wait
for that raccoon or bear to make its entrance.

You are late, they say.

The bear winds up his organ
and invites you to dance.

Even Better Than That

Less than a century of tragedies, and of course we fumble, we've
learned to fly and feel safe 20,000 miles up in the sky—

O, sunbeam, sling us a shot of a million butterflies—

    and we shall thaw, we shall lift in doubt, in fever, when
that very moment of life-death is in doubt, a billion times.

Not by the Skin, by the Teeth

Caught drunk once more on a wild sailboat ride, staring out into the ocean's salmon-streaked horizon.

Who says it should have been otherwise. You recognize that all this and all those theories are seductive, bold-handed, voiced precisely; and yet who sent you this message?

That poem I read the other night after listening to the woods and you sleeping in the garden with the worms.

It's all fractal, you said, almost mockingly, pulling the creatures from your hair. Watch where the arrow flies on another fine day, you said.

A Daisy Chain of Paper Stars.

Step lightly on those toes.

    They are the source

        of your strength,

           your breath

                asleep in the sun.

                    Pristine as you are,

                smooth as a fine day,

            and you wonder why

        the eels bite

        all your tenter-

hooks.

They're used to ghosts, you say,

    stepping lightly

on the clouds,

then unrolling them

into a solemn prayer.

Shall we sit on that carpet

and ride it out into the sun?

All the trees in the world,

old as they are,

have sailed away to Byzantium,

on the Wang River

in Yunnan,

or swim with the trans-

lucent eels

near those

hydrothermal vents

over a crust of

carbonic pleasures.

A Confluence of Gods

There she stands in all her radiance, as always unannounced; late, yet still blooming. Why this apple tree choses to be the one that collides, eludes me.

Posterity would say, What would you have done if, through no design of your own, you let it slip?

All that time, workers were walking to the factory, while you, in your mind at least, were gratefully dancing your way toward destiny. It's a breath-taker all right, a manifest destiny if you will, simply a breath away from the hustle and wrestle of the everyday, or the one who holds the course.

[insert wild animal here ...]

It is indeed strange, phantasmal almost, that they all meet at the confluence of the sun.

O apple tree, where my mother is buried and my hound looks out to the mountain, shower us in that domed umbrella of light as the walls creep across the hills from here to Galilee.

On a Scale of One to Fish

O to be desired, and to be desired back so easily.

Yes, I know the timpani rolls.

The crashing cymbals of reality.

We were jaded in the scale, just above where the fleshy part dwells, or perhaps, on another scale, we had found the best flesh.

A sunrise always helps.

Congressional Hearings

As such, the dictum states,
and in this I mean, obviates

a scant piece of evidence to prove,
without the shadow of a doubt,

that—(and there's evidence
we all sink or swim

with our nether regions, sir)—
the earth endures. It's a mainstay

of life on this planet, madam.
All right, so let us tally high

and ho, the dictum states:
Where is all this newfound evidence?

It's all hidden up your sleeve, sir.
I make no attempt to try and possess it.

We serve the common folk after all, sir.
Tenscore, I wish I could say,

but it's only been four.
Don't get me wrong.

Being dead has its advantages.
There's evidence to prove it.

Self, of course, is revealed
through self-less-ness, sir.

From Here to Galilee

... and the sardines are soft yet firm,
their skins have quietly braised in history.

Copious Knowledge

The art of dance beats in the wrist; so much so, I forgot about going home to the tree of knowledge to coo amongst the Doves of Windermere; yet, in plain sight, at every moment, gregarious eyes. That expansion into black as white or white as black, or, as has been intimated in the literature of the old gods: Drop thy leaning glance upon me. To sire, means I would sire you, and that, in plain sight of every moment.

Crab Nebula

And, in that instant, she listens to your plea,
hastens the settings of the moon,
an autumn voyager; the question clear,

the answer deep within; all that time spent
in front of the window, all those forecasts,
and the signs, the bundles of swallows,

the ragged lines of crows,
or the geese colluding in the hedgerows,
the rodents zigzagging all over forest and meadow,

and the late bumblebees digging into the moss:
truly exorbitant, those last droplets of honey,
and sweeter still than most.

Outside of the Ten I Owe You

What's my rank and file? you asked.

I heave sacks onto crates and cranes, I said.

Naturally, my mind wanted to chime in, so I actually said: You'll never be missing me.

And you, in your sly way, one eyebrow arching across like Spock, draw your mind across your eye.

Did you see the green flags on the hill?

They are all just trees, you said mockingly.

Which part of the code don't you get? you said.

Just wait, I said haltingly.

Outside of the ten I owe you, there's still the matter of the cat and the crate and the wedding cake.

A Year of Icelandic Ash

Reykjavík, day one:

Celtic coffee cups tumble, Nordic cake dishes shatter in their cerulean frosting; an Inuit elderberry sauce lazily cakes the fridge. An ancient accident ascends to the ceiling. The spiders follow.

Outside, a puffy cloud of volcanic ash salts and peppers the mountain's curves.

Is this Loki stirring his demon gazpacho?

No sound right now, only light from the ridge: a reflection of that moment for John Lennon; and imagine, Yoko was here too.[1]

She too ethereally shimmers over our shallow icy waters, then, flapping, squawks and howls like an Arctic tern.

day twenty:

We whirl ourselves away under a sun that burns behind a mountain. Rock ptarmigan tonight, roasted in duck fat and a lemon-parsley velouté. We discover wild arctic thyme along the road in tufts willing to be plucked for tomorrow's lamb stew with potatoes.

Gray hares scatter into the underbrush. A white-tailed eagle circles beneath a rose-crown of cirrus. Lurking on snow-flecked telephone wires, Freyja chuckles and caws with Odin's ravens.

An old man reels in his empty fishing nets.

A young man lets his sheep loose into the thickening snow.

day forty-three:

Three other people in the village church sing praises and hallowed-be-thy-names. The vicar bows in his ruffled collar; he sings to the good lord in his creaky *tungamal.*[2]

A woman rises from the congregation and squeaks in the tongues of wargods and lovegods. She is modeled on an ancient lovegod; she atones. The folk bow and kowtow.

For an instant the vicar looks up to the ceiling. He thinks he sees Freyja beckoning him into the light with a handful of sheep's sorrel and a shapely bosom. He thinks she is shaping the future for him, for us.

The stillness is palpable; the light, a promising pristine.

day one hundred and fifteen:

Pale carnations on sale in Mosfellsbaer from Kenya's Lake Naivasha. Not a breath of wind in the sky, clumps of frost cling to lichen, eyes flicker within the canyons.

Aren't we all collectors of beacons from the other side—or the underside, where all those other conversations reside.

Above the chimneys and their plumes, aurorae.[3] Rán and Ægir summon their crosswinds, and for an instant, everything vanishes into a blue haze.

day one hundred and seventy-five:

Tightening in/toughening up/stretching out. Drawing brass corset strings; always wary to perch on the ladder and paint everything in the hundred-fold of you in your new tectonic plate.

Still, Freyja points to the bare arches of the roof. Undercooked, she says, meaning we didn't consider the very edges of our habitat.

A lone seagull gives us the once-over. Later, he reappears at the barbeque and pilfers a steak straight off our hot coals. A flurry of volcanic ash settles on his beak and he sneezes, but he whisks the meat away over an enflamed and stinging ocean.

40

Streaks of blood and a fatty smear leave a trail leading straight down the fjord where the young salmon move from fresh to salt water. Waves whip up into frothy peaks; sea lions plunge into the deep.

Like a child, Njord[4] gathers seashells, driftwood and seaweed and apparently casts them haphazardly ashore.

day two hundred and one:

Fogged in on all sides.

Thor was on the warpath again, just like in his old days.

After several draughts of wild-thyme-infused mead, the sky
seemed to bend toward the antipodes; a Viking sunstone[5]
lead us through the thickest fog where the winged serpents
writhe. Still, Fog and her daughter, Mist, dream on in their own
voluptuousness, encircling and surrounding simply everything
until it appears there is nothing else but pale blue curves.

And then the blues quickly push us toward the peak. From
here we see the salmon spawn, keel and glide into the water—
dissolving, separating into their retrospectively paired strands,
splitting apart, dividing, finally reconfiguring, bubbling,
foaming, until, once again, they seek the salt of the open ocean.

How could we not be seafaring creatures? asks Aegir, god of
wind and sea.

day two hundred and ninety-eight:

There were rumblings of us reaching Valhalla arm in arm, bursting into the mead chamber and clamoring for an audience of out-to-pasture warriors.

There was also talk of discovering Vinland[6] and shaving our heads as clean as unmolded clay in the fashion of the ancient fey.

But, without running off at the mouth, in those days, he was a bastion of solidity, or so he thought, when headed into battle with the berserker mushroom running amok.

Is this what they call the dance of fire? Didn't we become human when we learned to cook?

And then there was that baptism by fire and flame.

day two hundred and nighty-nine:

And again we scour the shores for our sleep.

Throw yourself out of yourself like a god, you scream, and I dream with hardly any effort at all, between the very first and most prescient warning signs:

the swirling yoke of the seafowl on the backs of whales, the lone raven coasting on an updraft, a troll hibernating deep within the mountain who turns to scratch his nose.

But beware: just like the gods, he sleeps with one eye open.

43

Subliminal Message

The left hand turns the key, unattached, artfully. The other sits in his pocket, rubbing coins. Behind, the universe is streaming in, unpacked in all that matter. The mice are playing in the larder searching for wholegrain flour, the cat is sniffing something in the breeze. Multiple moons cast their wary glances, autumn fields are ripe in berries. The bear ambles along as is his lot on a Thursday night. Each instant is a reality for him, each past, nothing more than a dream; mostly it's the shrill sound of the gray tree frog that stirs him—oh, but nothing can keep him from the garbage, the discarded nappies, a scratching of leftover andouille, and all the plastics in their glossy underbellies. Once the corn has been reaped, then the sun, then when the fields are bare and unbearable lightness rises from those leftover, it's as if a frozen shadow sweeps across the earth, and all that is left is sleep.

Spectral Activity

Trying to reach out
to a precise location,
to a fingerpoint—
a helix that cuts off at the light,

switches on the world,
gives us god-thoughts;
all those evenings
in cafés staring out;

all those soundless steps,
straight ahead into
headlights with
that nugget of faith;

all those god-thoughts
sprinkled with cinnamon
and brown sugar, the firm belief
in something else, in some-

thing spectral, other-
worldly, something
along death's path
in a patch of fog;

see all the brows
furrowed on the shore,
the great wave
of hair.

The Great Wave of Hair

... how they came
from the other side
... to mate
and spawn and breed

Tantamount to Success

Take a dragon heart,
smother it in a thick béchamel,
preferably with slivers
of roasted almond, and bake!

Spectral Analysis

Down at the port where the ribbons flow on a Friday night the pubs are crowded at five, the old skippers congregate, drifting greedily into their odd banter: who caught the most frightening fish, who came face to face with the deep in the eye of a giant squid, or barely escaped that battering from an angry blue whale. Imagine what else they go on about: long time coming, storm cloud on the horizon, beneath the weather, then above. Here come the mackerel, the herring, the scores of transatlantic cod. Once this place was loaded with sardines in wooden barrels and sailed from here across the world. The fish could be scooped up by almost any hand—they came from as far as Siberia, followed by all the seagulls and one hundred years of frostbite. Take this very can, over one hundred years old herself, dented and rusted, the metals seep in, but the oil (imported from the Cretan islands) is still a thick emulsion and when you bite in, the salt crystals crackle and fizz on your tongue, and the sardines are soft yet firm; their skins have quietly braised in history, touched by cosmic background radiation.

★

All's well with you, you say. I would hand you some fragments, some cold evidence, how they were herded onto the boats, searing in pain from cable burns, or those who died with a wire across their eyes, or the cut and scrape of their gills against cold steel; how they came from the other side of the planet to mate and spawn and breed where the most vital and vibrant river finds its source.

Your Version of Adamant

A young, lithe version of you, all lashes and absinthe,
all black leather boots, eye makeup and a riding crop.

Here in the now, elsewhere too?
Didn't you say you order the world?

Aren't you he who apportions the chores?
I might have forgotten you on our way to Samsara:

It's the longing that counts, the eyes behind the mascara;
are you ready to walk into that great wall of fire?

And his balls are aflame as he forms his cross,
bears his necklace of garlic as he strides hot coals.

We're not ready to go! he screams.
His assassins are a vaudeville act, something

like what seems to hurtle you away on the quick—
all that tumbling and juggling and spinning;

all that jostling and applauding, all that clearing-
the-throat for a whole aviary of puffed-up peacocks.

The King of Prussia is Drunk on Stars
(Weltvernumpft; or, How to Hand on the Crown)

The Colonial Rose

Here's another one of those alms
born from the heart of the Empire.

We had to sever it at the roots.
Come what may, this face-to-face is endearing.

Yes, outside these walls, you're all
headed into the wilds, you wildebeest youngfolk!

Here's to another round on the house!
Open those books, let us see all of your tracks

and treasures, your tax evasions, your hyper-
ventilations, your you-who're-in-the-know

evocations; I drown in them, you say,
but where there's a storm there's a fair-weather.

The Alphabet

Herds, herds of them jostling and jutting, cranking
and bonking, bust up but alive, thanks to the birds.

Where there's a will, eh? By the roadside
everything looks the same; but to look is not to see.

We think this is so old, but it's all here.
Something like night descends and we see a vague

specter crossing the path, enduring time. Tell me
you didn't just pull that one out of your sleeve.

53

A Sunrise Never Sleeps

In deep, deep in, knee-deep, the deep infusion
in the will to survive. Keep going, you're not even close,

throw your tropes into the ocean. I was with you
once, before I was you. All that malarkey of manifest

destiny—a southern sunrise, I believe. The deep,
a place of no respite, almost blind, much alive

and not stumbling or staggering in the dark, but vibrant
in its own infinity—oh those strange crustaceans near

the vent pipes, the spill of an interior earth. Don't trust
the royal decree. Someone wants to know why

you think differently, why you treasure your throne,
why behind the grid, everything comes so easily.

The Dysgenic Twist

No idea behind which god you stand, *Frère*.
Imagine a sudden leap of faith bursting

through the clouds—an incidental ray of sun-
shine, unless you left as I did, with the wo-

man in the meadow and the stars divided
among the seas; then dove in, fathomless,

eternally searching for their fragments.

55

The Untold Truths

Heaven forbid I should hand you my successor.
Your cling was unstable, like things that fall out

of water or water out of fish, you cling to
a metaphysical substance—a word in the water

to the unfound, the unrecorded, the un-purported;
all these theories based on loose evidence;

or the momentary shift of alliances, the crowd-
sourced field of daisies, buds in bloom, a beam

of moonlight filled with faeries, a jungle
colorized by Cezanne. The long look,

it seems is populated by sleek, unflinching
sea lions perched on the slippery rock of their choice—

with seaweed or without, they conspire not; or
did they, in their glossy, fatty-furry-way conjure

with it an ode of supreme silence?

This I Heard You Say

It was existence; it's a jungle out there.
All those realms of experience like a network

of arteries, this one bigger than the last; or
the course of the river, beginning at the source,

the immaculate third eye, the crystal of wisdom;
the untold held to account for all those woes,

the fracture split halfway down the globe. The
was and is, the where, the why-are-you-claiming-

the-age-of-reason, or the season: untold
Decembers back in the kitchen of last

summer where the warming chimes of the
wide-open spaces were like kings of old.

Conscription Theory

The last words from the surface of the sun
are brighter than should be permitted.

They are of the substance we call ethereal,
that other never-discovered element,

elemental in substance, unsubstantiated
in chemical trials; alternative theories abound,

from the hocus-pocus of the POTUS,
to an anonymous tribe living deep in the woods;

all theories are brighter than should be permitted.
Let us close here with these last words:

What is the difference between an obstacle
or an expression of attainment?

Conspiracy Theory 101

Upheld in all beliefs
and traditions, scarce,

but widely transmuted.
I know, a Scheherazade

of shipwrecks; bet upon
the first child, they say.

And you, you were difficult
to hold—every broken pane

in the house talked to you;
in March, you knew

the rain before it came;
you adored that sodden

terrain where old souls
rise smoking through

the leaves; you were
crying with happiness

in the deepest shade of love,
you seemed to be emerging

in chains of paper stars; perhaps,
one day we shall all experience

true history in the long-
hand of the sun.

More Naked Truths

... the objects fed upon themselves,
but no one ever mentions that ...

Fire Tattoo

From the underside of the world she emerged as an eel
out of the carcass of a waterlogged horse;

all her invisible powers just as they appeared
in that comic book. One string on her shoulder,

bullets hailing, and just as desperately as
she wanted to be (superfluous how?) ... listen,

we've loved the bureaucrat, and no doubt
the politician too—from the wafer in your

chocolate ice cream to the glacial air breathing
across our faces, we've been robbed—every

newspaper mutters it. Moses meant what he said.
Imagine this: you're not who you think you are at all.

Into the Uneven Edge

The crumbled fragments of wasps and flies, crushed shells, mangled legs, missing antennae, and all that follows.

A day in the life, after all.

Through this place, the hemlock trees stretch their fingertips, and when we enter this non-human realm, many centuries flash by—who knows how many.

See, you recognize yourself.

Past lives, perhaps?

Me? I walk across my bedroom floor losing sight, knowing I acquire a little in my own time.

The road is heavy to carry in your own name.

The Brainchild of One Hundred Lullabies

Who would do that? suddenly someone said in the middle of their breathing exercises. Was that an ancient Indian wisdom?

The worst of it, is that I'm sure this has been written elsewhere; you don't want to wear that uniform, unable to swim, since that heavy fabric pulls you down.

As we know from the future, a blue moon will rise again straight out of the ashes, and a four-headed eagle will fly toward high-culture.

From your high chair, the angels cannot save you.

All That Binds You

I. *Blustering Wind*

End of September, ferocious rains; how long
ago were our poor souls entwined? The song
still rings in my ears, such certainties we faced

as we drifted by on a barge. That certain some-
thing, was it ether or fire? Then later, all these
misfortunes and the rational self kicked in.

Now the crickets squeak; the tender barking
behind the fence; the kids hop down their hillock
made of plastic on the way back from school.

The music of our age is all aflutter in nothingness,
we exquisite children of litter, of rust, of shriveled
hedges, rushing into that relish of but.

Manhunting with all our gods and demons. What,
you ask, is the worst insult of all? The latter
is the answer. Of course, we'll never know

for sure, but how can we endure from seeing
into the future. Of course everything is a metaphor.
How else can you escape the inescapable? ...

II. *Dreams of Wynter*

Falling into the years malevolently, sealed in cryogenic chambers; all those frightening absences, then it arrives without warning. I didn't even ask why you were here, or why your eyes held everything in multiples, or of the flashes in the room.

Outside, nothing save a few clouds.

God save us, you said, hiding behind a handful of carnations. You vanished into a halo for a moment, cast aside all vitriol.

We're privileged, of course, you said. True lives hold up to much more than this.

Stripped of my wits, I looked out the window and saw a solitary monkey swinging past the friezes. An invincible hero, he seemed to me, braving the snow and the storm and the blustering wind.

The Last Sidekick

I felt distinguished, anchored and heavily antlered. I knew, also, in short, I would be butting up against stone. Remember how in our youth we traced our feet in all the dances, but our brains wandered easily. I'm not sure if it was lack of faith or conviction, or if the language of childhood condenses each long-winded myth into bite-sized morsels. Now our words sit under our fingernails; the best of it is all the smoke, the bubbles, the battered suitcases; the inflatable bed rising with responsibility and a bad conscience. Once upon a time, there were spectators and accomplices, and in that March together frantically in love, the sights, the conch shells, the cobbled lanes, the breathable voices; once upon a time we had no interest in such a fundamental question—no matter the prompting from relatives and friends.

We thought through the landscapes, the faces and gestures; the objects fed upon themselves, but no one ever mentions that. There's no recto or verso, the watch won't unwind itself. The distinguished in their panpipes and whistles, all those tradeoffs and affairs couldn't be counted in one sitting.

A Language of Madness

I'm content to sit by the lake.

Could you find a safer spot?

Here I am master of my fate. When I was still alive, I didn't think. Both eyes appeared closed, but one was blinking—oh and all that incense and heady perfume, the purring of cats, the cogs and wheels of the grandfather clock were crippling. My father never believed in lubrication, clearly.

Those who don't read or listen: how can we "spot" them?

Franzl on the Moonsoaked Path

They sleep deep in the vault
and when they emerge
they recognize no one.

The Volcanologist

Descended from heaven but rarely aware of the ill omens or the lethal brand on the screen, the smoke bombs in the corners. Credibility is only the fire that forged us. Unpronounceable for those who wish to say it, then slough through it, for those leaving and arriving, like the woodworm, we were born in a chest, we lit them up, we would slip them into the grassy yard, take deep breaths, then quietly ask,

From which star?

Unhand Me, You Cad

That secret life passed by lit by clouds; you woke up again, stirred in your fiery pillars, crossed land to edgeland with those innocent eyes; somewhere in the knees I felt it when you saw the city lights from the hills. As you descended into the dark, your cool hands pressed together. "That is my tree," you said, purring. "I want to be a tree like that," I said, whirling in my dizzy head.

That night, the great snows descended, here where the crossroads meet. The clouds became one and a white light burst across the sky. I was like a lump of clay in the road, you were like a peacock, preening, but half-petrified in fear. Hold me fast, you said, the great telescope on the other side of the earth runs through all waveforms of light, only to come out this side.

In a fit of fury, we left the city on the first bus out of town.

Eventually, we hit a neon sign on the outskirts, which read:

Get Your Mixed Metaphors Here!

A Greek Tragedy

Crows litter
the countryside
in their glossy feathers,

bunches of dry stems
emerge from the earth,
a few webs of plastic

cling on—little flags
pointing the way—
I cross the road,

my skin a bolt
of bleached fabric;
the old features

replaced by heavier,
hardened ones—

impressive as cast iron,
but walking in the dark
like a memory.

Such a Victorian

The bird that flutters reaches out
into time; knee-deep in nerve gas;

at the cemetery gates, the children play
like half-opened flowers on a breeze; but,

deep in the coffers beneath that layer of non-
sense all along the big rivers, the fishermen

stock themselves in a hefty dose of rum.
The ship sails on to Shanghai, and, like the silent

strokes of a whip; or the snake tongues that rise
from the sea; the insane iron eyes staring

from the keep; I hope the many-more of you
are blind like the singer in all his rose of hope;

that gathering of ruffled skirts, the approachable
neckline, the stars in the charts; those who wander

from a kiss, or in some insane way, close
up the iron holes so all we have is surface.

In the Dark Corner of a Field Again
(Nachahmung)

I.

Is choice a consistency?

He who wanders through the grass,
Confucius said, opens up the ends of the earth:

the apple-tree blossoms are luminous
as the green seas, pale as silver—
they sleep deep in the vault
and when they emerge
they recognize no one.

II.

The signs in our hearts
are the paths to our treadways,
the crisscross rivers of fragrance
and pheromones; half-muffled,
a bark—is there a guiding spirit?

III.

Who beats the quilts in silky beds
of reed, or like that choice consistency
in bread where the old moon
sacrifices almighty god,
where in the green vault
they're shaking out their linens—
or is this a sanctuary
that never arises?

IV.

They were let out before they started,
they stared into the corner of the field,
intent, intensely held in sway—
too much cement
pouring from their hearts—
so long to home,
but no, it doesn't end here.

V.

And now in the
peppertrees, in the reflections
of the dark waters
(and don't forget, inside,
the glass translucent with frost
never opens, jars, sketches,
encourages faces—
a mild wisdom to take away).

VI.

I wish I might quietly ask
how those towers were built,
why they're growling at everything
and how those shadows
with their raspy calls and
snow-powdered throats
can still get through—
and come home.

All the Roads Have Come

The silence that lives in the grass goes off into a room inside the rocket. Those foothills were good for the bowels and the words; just small words, just in case; amid all that is great, the small words are those that resound across the meadows, the woodland, through the inner and outer cities, dangling on the earlobe, spraying from the earth, surrounded by bees in all their collective fury or the atoms that vibrate your body to life; there's no end to the messages, they come from one planet to another.

They say, What? What should we say to the people on earth? Perhaps something like: We came here so suddenly.

Fiery Spaces

Shall we map out the world, pronounce those curious
names, flounder with our founder, astonish

and admonish. Walk through the door into Ingrid's
home-sweet-home? Shall we ally our tears in a sea

of sorrow? The baffler has his toil; am I
being reasonable? There's only one thing you know,

you say. Let's open up the world for a day.
Put your feet up. This is a soundproof mountain.

Harry Houdini

A cat scampers
through shrubs,
over leaves, out-

    side the blue-
    backed sky
    and the clatter

        of stones
        in the woods—
        further off

an engine growls.
What do you hold
in your hands?

    A pole to prod
    your way through
    the chicken wire?

        To beat off
        the starving bears?

Look down to
where solid matter
meets the floor,

    behind tabloids,
    registration numbers
    in election years,

or the hungry who die
by the millions,
even where em-

phatically magical folk
live, or the some-
timers, the marginalia—

those pretending
to hide in the interior;
quite often,

in fact, look back
into the bloodshot eye-
ball of time—

tree after tree
in our strange groves
where the wind

whistles questions
and a blue-backed sky
growls outside

in the sky-high
dwelling; sneers
in the mirrored glass,

and says, Shall we give
them the sun
or snuff out the stars?

Over the Snowfield

Burrowing into the mountain,
moving through that layer
of grass and green roots,
a little cluster of fungi passes.

They are somewhere, else-
where, perhaps behind
that juniper bush?
Would you offer your hand

to a tiny red flock
of cardinals? They'll be
heavy in the storm,
you say, all that crimson

has nowhere to go
but deep into the earth. And,
then you think of the meadow
by the shore where

the cherry trees grow,
where the crows are
acrobats in late autumn.
Once I saw a lone

hen cross the pasture,
pecking and cooing as
she went. Hell knows
what that clucking hen

thinks of flying, and all
those seeds moving
on to Patagonia, sharp,
little flecks of hot iron.

Franzl Lashed to the Railroad Tracks

Of course I wish to exist just like summer
and pave that road with more words.

Seeking a Publicist

You can sing for your crumbs, Odin:
The grass is still green in my golden belt,

you think: what an unspeakable world:

The Emperor swore to restore the balance,
all his great benevolence unfolding between his wings.

What a sublime world, he intimated,
raising a polka-dotted hankie to his lips.

You have been surrounded
by the dull and the obtuse,

the wafflers and the warblers,
the whine-whingers, the gin-and-tonic-ers,

but you know how to sing for your crumbs:
I hadn't had time to notice it before, but

the gods dish out to those who seek fame.
As soon as I have polished this up, maybe

while the weather is still nice and warm,
something to think about seriously.

To the Top of the Hill
on the Moonsoaked Path

Who wants to fight the deluge?
Score the first hat trick?
Find the sound in the hound?
Who wants that reign of terror?

Once, someone chose eternal law.
You declined at once.
You said, How can we meet
in Berlin on Thursday?

Franz said, Get ready to soar.
Know that every wave moves
toward the center. Now the clouds
roll in, unraveling the air currents.

The shore slips below, and gladly so.

It's a reprieve.

Someone chose you once,
but to no avail, every deep canyon
wanders, searches in all those forgotten
depths where there is a whole world,

but no fire ants among the roots:
smoke is sparse, but the message stands.
You'll have to tilt your head
way back to see the sky here.

More Overflow

Hand in hand full of hours, then the clocks
ticking, somewhere a chanson, Édith Piaf
perhaps? Do not go to that door. The rest-

aurants are all closing. Who was the first to say
her name? Your brother with the beheaded
tulips at the gate? They watched him enter

at the street, bewitched. Had his time truly
come, Franzl? Yes, I know it was then
she decided to bloom. And you?

You lay your ear to the floor,
listening for her train to roll in as if you
could have waited at every bench on any gate.

Dying Daffodil

Someone said there exists this other place—
in a word, a place like none other, soaked

in heavenly light, where deep down in the water
you can see where the darkness lives.

Who can cross this, you say. What ferryman
follows at my heels? Surely I am not one of

the forgotten, one of the numb or deaf;
I know you want me to kiss the lips of the flowers;

it would go halfway to paying off my debt.
Of course I wish to exist just like summer

and pave that road with more words, then
enter the next that exists somewhere out

there, and perch there under the apple tree,
and to turn my eye to everything within.

Spell for Hallowed Ground

Whichever words you speak,
linger on the dark blue eyes.

This may open the lids
of the dead one.

When you peel back her eyes
an even stranger blue rematerializes.

You know these waters.
You know those stones.

On the Other Side of the Fence

From whom did she get the starring role?

Dissidents

Unfurled, who knows where to?
shall we lead them away?

Some things are better left unsaid, you said, imbibing a strange
drink—green, and with a maraschino.

Would the fish flock to join him? you said.
They'll flock to those Lazarus eyes, and that

which is concealed small in the lattice of that
oh-so-human skull. Your silence smothered

much of my talk, syllable by syllable.
it was like blood and part of the sacrificial

ritual. Through the trough, we went, O Lord.
One shall not be led astray. Let every

mouth stand open and empty, let a word
like this enter and swing free like pendulum.

I shall dig myself toward you, they say.
We shall make un-truths truths, they say.

Let a dying moth fly to her flame, they say.
Do you hear the digging? the dredging?

The logging? the extinct languages?
Picture one of these languages in all of its

coarseness, picture a whistle that can be
a word, a word that can be a legend.

97

Of Too Much Talk

Water was scarce that year; that which there was often murky—it all reflected in the mouth and in the eye—that much holds true, or so I've heard.

There are so many constellations held dear to us, and not just here, but all that grows alongside the window. One gaze leads us though. We have no concourse.

Where your eye is, there you grow.

Coup d'État

Hast thou fallen away?
has the same thing forgotten us
that has us ensnared?
Praised be thou,
and for whom shall we sing?

Over and over,
that "Old Man Crow" song?
Heaven is enraged
from earth to sky!

I am a baffled man.
(Well, the world today
has its bloody limits. Just post
your drivel and babble.)

Foolish, foolish man,
driving words like nails,
taking all the appleseed.
The flood and flow
of good cider knows

your were just beginning to open up.
Your words dried up at half-past three,
but I wish you to knowingly
enter my kingdom.

All the crows have lined up in a row.

99

Where are all my dragonslayers now?
All seeking their own treasures, yes?
Before you lay me open,
must I sing
for my wine?

In a Seaswell

We were
swimming
and any fool
would have seen
this was an endless
pool; it grew on the edge
of the world, it hung,   it dangled.
Do you still recall that song?
You didn't need   to sing;
you reappeared just
before the wind   t o o k
over. You plucked it
from the light
and released it into
the ocean—that
bright container
which no fool
has ever
s e e n.

Co-Star

More light, please, more light.

I wake up with a splitting headache. I need to be bathed in a deep-in-the-bones warmth.

What was that code word we needed to get over the border? That wasn't that time in Tuscany, was it?

The whirring of the crickets, the names and the amens, the great benevolence. From whom did she get the starring role? From whence, you mean, dear, don't you? The great adolescence raising the Tower of Babel. May we lay ours down for those who failed to return. What pandemonium. You must go, you said. That one is a precise as crystal. Here, a souvenir.

Now you have them both.

Franzl, after Eating the Trifle

... all the love letters from Normandy
with your name in my hand
from the mouth of the future.

Unctuous

At the end of the road, I should think people keep things to themselves; always a path goes further into the woods. When you see those in the next clearing, if you've crossed the gullies and lagoons, not quite the land beyond the mountain, but a deep wandering. And, as you go, remember those days in Prague, all the love letters from Normandy with your name in my hand from the mouth of the future.

Once before, I unthought all those thoughts, I stood at the bottom of the rapids, touched them in all my fingers—their will-o'-the-whispering of morning, trout laced with all those veins of silver pushing upstream, wholly mad, wholly real at the river's source.

How Many Have Eaten Here?

At the roll of the dice, he said, a handful per night, hard to tell with all those light conversations and their amphetamines. He was talking about the heavy-lipped, long-legged, deep in bed without names; and in spite of it all, sewn under the skin of his hands, a glimmer of eyes passing overhead.

Absurd, he said, all those bottlenecks.

Who says we have to be world's backbone?

Come Dancing With Me

Where are you headed with all that cargo? One often heard of those who made it. The messages filter back over the years, sometimes this way.

He eyed me with a caterpillar resting over his socket. I could almost see that caterpillar smoking a cigarette after sex.

All mankind, the caterpillar said, walk straight into metaphors like walls. Within these winding hills you should be able to get something straight. And it's because I'm positioned at a curve, I should know.

Let the burden carry you toward me.

I'm light on my feet. ★

Under Fire

Fill the entire mirror.

It's never night when you die,
winter still lives in the grass;

There we go, picking ourselves up. Grass
is never at rest, let alone last year's straw;

don't eye yourself in that angry green, begin
by astonishing her and know that you are in

her hands, in the beauty of her deep waters
for over two years of your life. Once there were

both woman and man and no one wooed anyone;
these last two years are the weeds in which

you believe. Life and death begins at the
hearth—upend the notion, taste that stringent

bitter, the red aperitif with an orange slice,
the darkness and the richness side by side.

Roll up your sleeves.

Your days are numbered.

A Wine-Bearing Grape

At the end of that chain of refutations, a snowy evening in the hills, and lovely beings settle in their gloomy chambers.

Blind pride opens up.

Wasn't it you? someone says.

This is not for the kingdom, another advises.

Both of you are sleeping, says a third.

She has that inward movement in her eyes: wild, animal-like. We notice her hair—frizzled, frizzy anyway; it answers just part of the question.

There's nothing like these terraces at midnight.

Acknowledgements

Much appreciation to the editors of the following journals in which these poems previously appeared.

Willow Springs: "Fire Tattoo"

Ink, Sweat and Tears (UK): "Such a Victorian"

Survision Magazine (Ireland): "Copious Knowledge," "On a Scale of One to Fish," and "Riptide"

Mudlark (*Mudlark Flash* No. 159): "Culture"

Okay Donkey: "Spectral Analysis"

Madswirl: "Conspiracy Theory 101"

Gargoyle: "A Confession of Sorts" and "Trash Nebula"

Midway Journal: "Shards of Air"

St. Petersburg Review: "Hallowed Ground"

Beltway Review: "Split Your Skull, Monster," "The Volcanologist," and "Even Better Than That"

spoKe 9: "Come Dancing with Me"

Book of Matches: "Over the Snowfield"

The Fortnightly Review (France): "A Greek Tragedy," "Come Dancing with Me," "Seeking a Publicist," and "Harry Houdini"

Clockwise Cat: "Spectral Activity" and "Not By the Skin, By the Teeth"

First Literary Review-East: "Tantamount to Success"

Voice & Verse Poetry Magazine (Hong Kong): "All the Roads Have Come" and "Dying Daffodil"

Sensitive Skin: "From a Hotel Window," "Congressional Hearings," and "Subliminal Message"

Earlier versions of poems from this collection were first performed on *Lit Balm*, the literary livestream reading series (www.litbalm.org).

Notes

"In the Dark Corner of a Field" is for P and K.

"A Year of Icelandic Ash" is for the *huldufólk*.

1. The Imagine Peace Tower, a memorial to John Lennon from his widow, Yoko Ono, located on Viðey Island in Kollafjörður Bay near Reykjavík, Iceland. Installed in 2007, it consists of a tall tower of light, projected from a white stone monument that has the words "Imagine Peace" carved into it in 24 languages.
2. Literal: "tongue-mouth;" trans: "language."
3. Disturbances in the magnetosphere caused by the solar wind.
4. Freyja's disgruntled father.
5. Possibly the mineral cordierite or Icelandic spar. A theory exists that the sunstone had polarizing attributes and was used as a navigational instrument by sailors in the Viking Age; use of which was considered the domain of those endowed with magic.
6. Vinland was an area of coastal North America explored by Vikings. Leif Erikson landed there around AD 1000, nearly five centuries before the voyages of Christopher Columbus.

"Co-Star" is for Marlene Dietrich.

"Crab Nebula" is for Emily.

"Under Fire" is for the people of Ukraine.

The Author

Marc Vincenz is a poet, fiction writer, translator, editor, musician and artist. He has published over 30 books of poetry, fiction and translation. His more recent collections include *The Little Book of Earthly Delights*, *There Might Be a Moon or a Dog*, *39 Wonders and Other Management Issues*, *The Pearl Diver of Irunmani*, and *A Splash of Cave Paint*. His work has been published in *The Nation, Ploughshares, Raritan, Colorado Review, Washington Square Review, Fourteen Hills, Willow Springs, World Literature Today, The Notre Dame Review, The Golden Handcuffs Review, The Los Angeles Review of Books*, and many other journals and periodicals.

His translation of Klaus Merz' selected poems, *An Audible Blue*, won the 2023 Massachusetts Book Award for Translated Literature. He is publisher and editor of MadHat Press and publisher of *New American Writing*, and lives on a farm in western Massachusetts where there are more spiny-nosed voles, tufted grey-buckle hares and *Amoeba scintilla* than humans.

Other Books by Marc Vincenz

Poetry

The Propaganda Factory, or Speaking of Trees

Mao's Mole

Gods of a Ransacked Century

Behind the Wall at the Sugar Works (a verse novel)

Beautiful Rush

Additional Breathing Exercises

This Wasted Land and Its Chymical Illuminations (annotated by Tom Bradley)

Becoming the Sound of Bees

Sibylline (illustrated by Dennis Paul Williams)

The Syndicate of Water & Light

Leaning into the Infinite

Here Comes the Nightdust

Einstein Fledermaus

The Little Book of Earthly Delights

A Brief Conversation with Consciousness (illustrated by Sophia Santos)

There Might Be a Moon or a Dog

39 Wonders and Other Management Issues

The Pearl Diver of Irunmani

A Splash of Cave Paint

Coalition No. 9 (Almost a Novel) (illustrated by Jake Quatt)

The Form of Time: New and Selected Poems

Spells for the Wicked (illustrated by Sophia Santos)

Limited Editions and Chapbooks

Benny and the Scottish Blues (illustrated by Dareen Dewan)
Genetic Fires
Upholding Half the Sky
Pull of the Gravitons
An Alphabet of Last Rites

Translations

Kissing Nests by Werner Lutz
Nightshift / An Area of Shadows by Erika Burkart and Ernst Halter
A Late Recognition of the Signs by Erika Burkart
Grass Grows Inward by Andreas Neeser
Out of the Dust by Klaus Merz   117
Secret Letter by Erika Burkart
Lifelong Bird Migration by Jürg Amann
Unexpected Development by Klaus Merz
An Audible Blue: Selected Poems (1963–2016) by Klaus Merz
Casting a Spell in Spring by Alexander Xaver Gwerder

Fiction

Three Taos of T'ao, or How to Catch a White Elephant
City of Lemons